BIOGRAPHIES *of the* NEW AMERICAN NATION

GEORGE WASHINGTON, THOMAS JEFFERSON, FREDERICK DOUGLASS, AND MORE

BIOGRAPHIES *of the* NEW AMERICAN NATION

GEORGE WASHINGTON, THOMAS JEFFERSON, FREDERICK DOUGLASS, AND MORE

Edited by Sherman Hollar

Britannica®
Educational Publishing
IN ASSOCIATION WITH

ROSEN

Published in 2013 by Britannica Educational Publishing
(a trademark of Encyclopædia Britannica, Inc.)
in association with Rosen Educational Services, LLC
29 East 21st Street, New York, NY 10010.

Distributed exclusively by Rosen Educational Services.
For a listing of additional Britannica Educational Publishing titles, call toll free (800) 237-9932.

First Edition

Britannica Educational Publishing
J.E. Luebering: Director, Core Reference Group, Encyclopædia Britannica
Adam Augustyn: Assistant Manager, Encyclopædia Britannica

Anthony L. Green: Editor, Compton's by Britannica
Michael Anderson: Senior Editor, Compton's by Britannica
Andrea R. Field: Senior Editor, Compton's by Britannica
Sherman Hollar: Senior Editor, Compton's by Britannica

Marilyn L. Barton: Senior Coordinator, Production Control
Steven Bosco: Director, Editorial Technologies
Lisa S. Braucher: Senior Producer and Data Editor
Yvette Charboneau: Senior Copy Editor
Kathy Nakamura: Manager, Media Acquisition

Rosen Educational Services
Jeanne Nagle: Senior Editor
Nelson Sá: Art Director
Cindy Reiman: Photography Manager
Karen Huang: Photo Researcher
Brian Garvey: Designer, Cover Design
Introduction by Jeanne Nagle

Library of Congress Cataloging-in-Publication Data

Biographies of the new American nation: from George Washington to Frederick Douglass/edited by
Sherman Hollar.—1st ed.
      p. cm.—(Impact on America: collective biographies)
Includes bibliographical references and index.
ISBN 978-1-61530-686-2 (library binding)
1. United States—History—1783-1865—Biography—Juvenile literature. I. Hollar, Sherman.
E302.5.B56 2013
973.4—dc23

                                                                        2011045403

Manufactured in the United States of America

CONTENTS

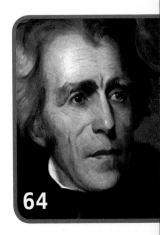

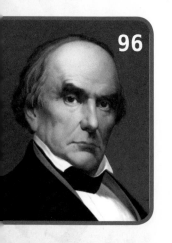

96

108

120

INTRODUCTION

The American Revolutionary War brought forth an independent nation known as the United States. Once the fighting was over and freedom declared, the job of forming and sustaining the "more perfect union" envisioned in the Preamble to the U.S. Constitution landed squarely on the shoulders of the fledgling country's citizens. The stories of these men and women are an important part of U.S. history. This book presents the biographies of several statesmen, explorers, warriors, and social reformers who helped shape the new American nation.

A number of revolutionary leaders gained important positions within the new federal government, including the presidency. In the latter group were George Washington, John Adams, and Thomas Jefferson. The nation's first president, Washington had proven himself a patriot as commander-in-chief of the Continental Army, then as the officer who oversaw the writing of the Constitution. Adams and Jefferson each had served under Washington—as vice president and secretary of state, respectively—before being elected president themselves. All three brought their personal and political beliefs to bear on the evolving U.S. government.

Among those who built the New American Nation were the presidents, including George Washington (center) and (clockwise) John Adams, James Madison, John Quincy Adams, Martin Van Buren, James Tyler, James Polk, William Harrison, Andrew Jackson, James Monroe, and Thomas Jefferson. **MPI/Archive Photos/Getty Images**

Other statesmen guided the United States toward its unique brand of democracy through persuasion and compromise. James Madison, John Jay, and Alexander Hamilton urged the pursuit of liberty through majority rule in essays that together are known as *The Federalist Papers*. In 1830 Senator Daniel Webster spoke eloquently (and at great length) in defense of the Constitution and the power of the federal government, which made him a national hero in the process. When tariffs and the subject of slavery were creating a serious rift between northern and southern states, Henry Clay repeatedly championed compromise legislation that kept the nation united for decades before the country erupted in civil war.

Expansion was a crucial element in the development of the new American nation. In 1804 President Thomas Jefferson sent Meriwether Lewis and William Clark on a westward expedition to explore territory recently acquired in the Louisiana Purchase and establish a path to the Pacific Ocean. The journey was also meant to establish ties with Native American tribes. Shoshone maiden Sacagawea joined the expedition as an interpreter. With her assistance, Lewis and Clark were able to gain the help from Western Shoshone tribes that made the completion of their mission possible.

Not all interactions with Native Americans were as successful. Anger at the loss of land to white settlers resulted in native uprisings, led by Indian chiefs such as Tecumseh and Osceola, throughout the 1800s. Relations between whites and African Americans at this time were also troublesome, to say the least. Nat Turner led a slave revolt in 1831 Virginia, which strengthened the intensity of the arguments on both sides of the slavery debate until the matter reached a boiling point during the American Civil War.

The treatment of groups such as Native and African Americans was protested by social reformers of the age. Chief among these reformers were the abolitionists, who were against slavery. William Lloyd Garrison, a leading abolitionist, used the power of his newspaper, the *Liberator*, to spread his anti-slavery message. The work of former slave and brilliant speaker Frederick Douglass also helped put an end to slavery in the United States.

It is safe to say that the personal lives of these and other leading U.S. figures were influenced by historic events that occurred as their country grew and prospered, and vice versa. Their stories are truly the stories of the new American nation.

CHAPTER 1

GEORGE WASHINGTON

Many U.S. presidents have been honored for their great achievements. George Washington's achievements have distinguished him as the Father of His Country. Washington was commander-in-chief of the Continental Army during the American Revolution, chairman of the convention that wrote the U.S. Constitution, and the first president of the United States. He led the people who transformed the United States from a British colony into a self-governing nation. His ideals of liberty and democracy set a standard for future presidents and the entire country.

Washington was born in Westmoreland County, Va., on Feb. 22, 1732. He was the eldest child of Augustine and Mary Ball Washington. His father owned plantations, businesses, and mines. After his father died in 1743, George lived with his half brother Lawrence at an estate on the Potomac River called Mount Vernon. George learned how to survey (measure) areas of land and to farm.

At age 16 Washington joined a group sent to survey unknown lands on the Virginia

Portrait of General George Washington, depicted upon his steed at the conclusion of the American Revolution. Washington's ardent patriotism led him to be named the first president of the United States. **Bob Thomas/Popperfoto/Getty Images**

13

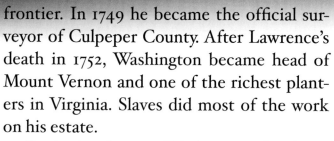

frontier. In 1749 he became the official surveyor of Culpeper County. After Lawrence's death in 1752, Washington became head of Mount Vernon and one of the richest planters in Virginia. Slaves did most of the work on his estate.

Beginning in 1754 Washington fought in the French and Indian War. He eventually became commander of all Virginia's troops. Washington also served in the House of Burgesses, Virginia's assembly of representatives. In 1759 he married Martha Dandridge, a widow with two children. The couple had no children together.

In 1775 Washington was elected to command the Continental Army. In the ensuing American Revolution, he proved a brilliant commander and a stalwart leader, despite several defeats. With the war effectively ended by the capture of Yorktown (1781), he resigned his commission and returned to Mount Vernon (1783). He was a delegate to and presiding officer of the Constitutional Convention (1787) and helped secure ratification of the Constitution in Virginia. When the state electors met to select the first president (1789), Washington was the unanimous choice. John Adams was elected vice president. Washington was inaugurated into office on April 30, 1789.

The newly formed U.S. government consisted of a legislative branch, the Congress; a judicial branch, the Supreme Court; and an executive branch, which was headed by

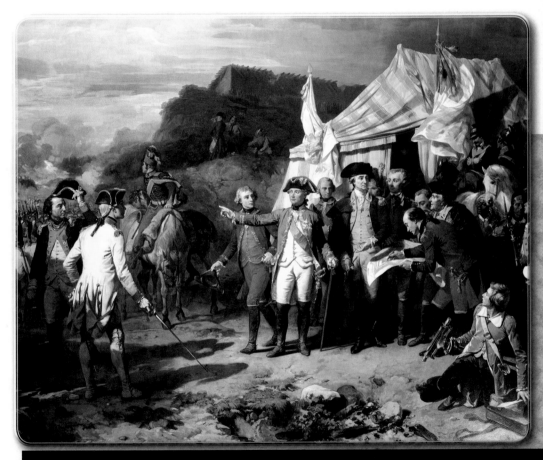

General Washington oversees the surrender of British General Cornwallis following the Siege of Yorktown. **The Bridgeman Art Library/Getty Images**

Washington and included his Cabinet. The first Cabinet members included Thomas Jefferson as secretary of state, Henry Knox as secretary of war, Edmund Randolph as attorney general, and Alexander Hamilton as secretary of the treasury. In 1790 Washington approved a permanent location for the U.S. capital on the Potomac River. The capital was moved from New York City to Philadelphia until the new capital was established.

During Washington's administration, the authority of the federal government was greatly strengthened. Washington and Hamilton chartered the Bank of the United States in 1791, and the federal government assumed responsibility for both national and state debts. Taxes were placed on imported goods and certain private property within the states, and money was deposited into the national treasury for paying debts. Also in 1791 the states ratified the Bill of Rights, the first 10 amendments to the Constitution, which granted U.S. citizens their basic rights.

Washington was reelected to a second term as president in 1792, with John Adams again serving as his vice president. Three new states were admitted to the United States during Washington's administration—Vermont in 1791, Kentucky in 1792, and Tennessee in 1796.

When war broke out between France and Great Britain in 1793, Washington decided that the United States should remain neutral in foreign affairs. Even though the United States owed France a debt for assistance in the American Revolution and promised to help France in any future conflicts, Washington felt that the United States was not prepared to enter another war so soon. The following year the U.S. government met its first serious domestic challenge with the Whiskey Rebellion in July 1794. Washington set a tax on whiskey to help pay the national debt. Farmers in western Pennsylvania who relied on the income from selling whiskey were outraged by the tax. These farmers resisted the tax by assaulting federal revenue officers. After negotiations between the federal government and the farmers failed, Washington dispatched local state militias and federal troops to quell the rebellion.

Washington's administration faced boundary disputes with the Native Americans on the western frontier, Great Britain in the

northeast and northwest, and Spain in the south. Settlers in the Ohio River Valley fought Native Americans over claims on the western frontier boundaries. Washington dispatched an army under the command of General Anthony Wayne to defend the settlements from the Native Americans. Wayne built a chain of forts from Ohio to Indiana to protect the settlements and, on Aug. 20, 1794, effectively ended Native American resistance in the region with a decisive victory at the Battle of Fallen Timbers in Ohio.

Washington authorized John Jay, chief justice of the Supreme Court, to negotiate boundary disputes with Great Britain. In the Jay Treaty, signed on Nov. 19, 1794, Great Britain and the United States negotiated the boundaries between the United States and British North America. Great Britain also granted the United States trading privileges with England and the British East Indies.

Thomas Pinckney, an American diplomat, was sent to Spain for negotiations concerning U.S. interests in Spanish-owned territories. Pinckney's Treaty, signed on Oct. 27, 1795, established the southern boundary of the United States at 31° N. latitude, opened the Mississippi River to U.S. trade through Spanish territories, and granted Americans a tax-free port in New Orleans.

When Washington's second term ended, he refused to run for a third term. He considered it unwise for one person to hold such a powerful position for so long. On March 4, 1797, John Adams was sworn in as president, with Thomas Jefferson as his vice president.

Washington retired to Mount Vernon, where he spent time with his family and resumed the management of his farms and estates. On Dec. 12, 1799, Washington returned home from a horseback ride through his farms in cold, snowy weather. He developed laryngitis and became weak and ill. He died two days later, on Dec. 14, 1799.

CHAPTER 2

JOHN ADAMS

As the first vice president and second president of the United States, John Adams was one of the founding fathers of the new nation. He is one of only two presidents whose signature appears on the Declaration of Independence. He applied his expert skills in foreign policy to secure diplomacy with Great Britain after the American Revolution and to avoid a potential war with France during his presidency. Adams was George Washington's vice president from 1789 to 1797, and then succeeded Washington as president, serving from 1797 to 1801. During his tenure in office, Adams led the country by upholding the values of liberty and democracy set forth in the U.S. Constitution.

Adams was born on Oct. 30, 1735, in Braintree (now Quincy), Mass. After graduating from Harvard College (now Harvard University) in 1755, he practiced law in Boston. On Oct. 25, 1764, Adams married Abigail Smith, a Congregational minister's daughter from Weymouth, Mass. The couple had four children: Abigail Amelia, John Quincy, Charles, and Thomas Boylston.

Active in the American independence movement, Adams was elected to the Massachusetts legislature and served as a delegate to the Continental Congress (1774–78), where he was appointed to a committee with Thomas Jefferson and others to draft the Declaration of Independence. From 1776 to 1778, he was appointed to many congressional committees, including one to create a navy and another to review foreign affairs. He later served as a diplomat in France, the Netherlands, and Great Britain. Working with Benjamin Franklin, he helped negotiate the 1783 Treaty of Paris that ended the American Revolution. Adams and Franklin, experienced and shrewd foreign diplomats, were credited with achieving favorable terms in the treaty with Great Britain, including the establishment of the western boundary of the United States at the Mississippi River.

In the first U.S. presidential election, Adams received the second largest number of votes and became vice president under Washington. In 1792 Washington was reelected president, with Adams remaining as vice president for another term.

In the presidential election of 1796, Adams ran as the Federalist candidate against

Drafters of the U.S. Declaration of Independence included Benjamin Franklin (left), *Thomas Jefferson* (seated, back), *and John Adams* (second from right). *The lives of Adams and Jefferson were politically intertwined.* **Stock Montage/Archive Photos/Getty Images**

Thomas Jefferson, the Republican candidate. Adams prevailed by a narrow margin of electoral votes (71–68) and was inaugurated into office on March 4, 1797. According to the Constitution, the presidential candidate with the second largest number of votes became vice president. Thus Jefferson was required to serve as Adams' vice president, even though both men were members of opposing political parties. (This law was later changed by the 12th Amendment to the U.S. Constitution, which ruled that presidential and vice presidential candidates had to be elected by individual ballots.)

When Adams began his presidency, the United States had been involved in a naval conflict with France since 1795. French privateers were attacking U.S. merchant vessels in the West Indies. In 1797 Adams sent three delegates to Paris to establish a peace settlement with France. When the U.S. delegates arrived, three French officials demanded a bribe of $250,000, payable to France's foreign minister, Talleyrand, before any negotiations could commence. Outraged by France's audacity, Adams ordered his delegates home and began preparing the U.S. military forces for a war with France. Adams referred to the three French officials as X, Y, Z in his correspondence to Congress, and the incident became known as the XYZ Affair.

Portrait of John Adams, second president of the United States. The Bridgeman Art Library/Getty Images

The Federalist-controlled Congress was eager for war with France after the XYZ Affair. Adams, however, was reluctant to declare war and sent another peace delegation to France in 1799. Although his fellow Federalists opposed this tactic, the negotiations with Talleyrand were successful, and the United States was spared from engaging in a costly war.

The XYZ Affair incited the Federalists in Congress to issue the Alien and Sedition Acts in 1798. To affirm their displeasure with France, Congress persuaded Adams to sign these acts into law. Aimed especially at French-born residents, the Alien Acts increased the waiting period for naturalization from 5 to 14 years. The acts also gave the president the authority to imprison or deport immigrants from an enemy nation who were considered to be a threat to the United States. The Sedition Act allowed federal authorities to incriminate anyone who published malevolent criticism directed at the U.S. government. By 1802, however, these acts had been either repealed or allowed to expire.

In the presidential election of 1800, Adams and Jefferson, by now bitter political adversaries, ran against each other. Jefferson won a majority of electoral votes (73–65) and took office on March 4, 1801. Despite the loss of the executive branch, Adams was determined to maintain his party's control of the judiciary. In January 1801, before his term expired, Adams placed several Federalist judges, clerks, and lawyers into key positions. He also appointed John Marshall as chief justice of the Supreme Court.

Adams refused to attend Jefferson's inauguration and instead returned home to Braintree. He spent his years of retirement with his family there. He wrote prolifically, on topics ranging from political commentary to farming, to his own memoirs. In 1812 he overcame his bitterness toward Jefferson, with whom he began a revealing correspondence. Adams also observed the rising political career of his son John Quincy, who became the sixth president of the United States in 1825.

Adams died in Braintree on July 4, 1826, the 50th anniversary of the Declaration of Independence. Jefferson died on the same day within hours of Adams.

CHAPTER 3

THOMAS JEFFERSON

Thomas Jefferson was the chief author of the Declaration of Independence and the third president of the United States. His remarkable public career also included service in the Continental Congress, as the country's first secretary of state, and as its second vice president. Among the founding fathers, Jefferson was the most eloquent proponent of individual freedom as the core meaning of the American Revolution.

Jefferson was born on April 13, 1743, in Shadwell, Va. His parents were Peter Jefferson, a land surveyor, and Jane Randolph, who was descended from one of the most prominent families in Virginia. Jefferson studied at the College of William and Mary in Williamsburg, Va., and gained admittance to the Virginia bar in April 1767. He returned to Shadwell in 1768 and designed his own home on an 867-foot (264-meter) mountain near Shadwell. He named his new estate Monticello, an Italian word meaning "little mountain." He married Martha Wayles Skelton on New Year's Day in 1772. The couple had six children. Martha

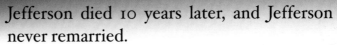

Jefferson died 10 years later, and Jefferson never remarried.

Jefferson depended on slave labor for the upkeep of Monticello. His ownership of slaves would become perhaps the most controversial aspect of his legacy. Even as he maintained that slavery contradicted the principles of freedom and equality upon which the United States was founded, he insisted that it was wrong for the federal government to end the practice. Further complicating the issue has been Jefferson's relationship with Sally Hemings, one of his house slaves. In 1998 DNA evidence revealed that Jefferson fathered at least one child with Hemings.

Jefferson was elected to the Virginia legislature in 1769. He became a strong supporter of American independence from Great Britain. In 1774 he wrote the influential A Summary View of the Rights of British America, stating that the British Parliament had no authority to legislate for the colonies. He served as Virginia's delegate to the Continental Congress in 1775 and 1776. In 1776 he was the main author of the Declaration of Independence. Jefferson wrote the famous lines that said "all men are created equal" and have the rights of "life, liberty and the pursuit of happiness."

Jefferson then returned to the Virginia legislature. There he proposed several important reforms to Virginia law. One important bill required the separation of church and state. It was called the Statute for Religious Freedom. After many years of debate the legislature passed the law in 1786. Jefferson also worked to make education available to all citizens.

In 1779 Jefferson was elected governor of Virginia. He faced fierce criticism the following year for his failure to organize effective opposition when British forces invaded the colony. In 1782 he reentered the Continental Congress. After the American Revolution ended, he replaced Benjamin Franklin as U.S. minister to France.

From 1790 through 1793 Jefferson was the first U.S. secretary of state, under President George Washington. Jefferson clashed with Alexander Hamilton, the secretary of the treasury. Jefferson and his supporters, called Republicans (or Democratic-Republicans), believed that the states should have the power to make their own decisions in most matters. Hamilton led the Federalists, who believed in a powerful central government. In 1796 Jefferson was elected vice president under President John Adams. As vice president, he opposed Adams' signing of the Alien and Sedition Acts (1798); the Virginia and Kentucky Resolutions, adopted by the legislatures of those states in 1798 and 1799, respectively, as a protest against the acts, were written by Jefferson and James Madison.

In 1800 both Jefferson and Aaron Burr ran for president against President Adams. Jefferson and Burr received the same number of electoral votes. The House of Representatives eventually chose Jefferson as the winner, and he was inaugurated into office on March 4, 1801.

The most important event of Jefferson's first term was the purchase of a large area of land known as the Louisiana Territory from France in 1803. Spain had ceded the Louisiana Territory to France in the Treaty of San Ildefonso in October 1800, and Jefferson and other U.S. leaders worried about losing access to the vital trade port at New Orleans. Jefferson sent delegates—among them James Monroe—to negotiate with French officials for the purchase of New Orleans. In a surprising turn of events, Napoleon I

A statue of Thomas Jefferson stands silent vigil within the Jefferson Memorial, in Washington, D.C. Shutterstock.com

offered to sell the entire Louisiana Territory, which stretched from the land west of the Mississippi River to the Rocky Mountains, to the United States for $15 million. In May 1803 U.S. delegates signed a treaty with Napoleon I for the Louisiana Purchase.

The western territories always intrigued Jefferson because he envisioned them as the future of the United States. To investigate the vastness of this newly acquired land in the West, he dispatched Meriwether Lewis and William Clark to blaze a trail through the Rocky Mountains to the Pacific Ocean. Their trail to the Pacific paved the way for future explorers and traders who sought to colonize the West.

Jefferson coasted to an easy victory in the presidential election of 1804 against the Federalist candidate, Charles Pinckney, but his second term in office was less successful than the first. The resumption of the Napoleonic Wars between Britain and France deeply hurt U.S. trade with Europe, and domestic agricultural and industrial markets suffered throughout his term.

After James Madison was inaugurated as the fourth president of the United States in

March 1809, Jefferson returned to Monticello. In 1812, after a long estrangement, he and John Adams were reconciled. The 158 letters they exchanged over the next 14 years became the most famous correspondence between two U.S. statesmen. Jefferson's last great project was the founding and designing of the University of Virginia in Charlottesville, which opened in 1825. Jefferson died at Monticello on July 4, 1826.

Considered a founding father of the United States, John Jay, like George Washington, was a man pursued by public office. For a quarter of a century after the start of the American Revolution he was given diplomatic missions, appointed to high offices, and elected to others. Although at first opposed to the idea of independence for the American colonies, fearing it would lead to mob rule, once the Revolution began Jay became one of its strongest supporters. As first chief justice of the Supreme Court of the United States from 1789 to 1795, he established important judicial precedents.

Jay was born in New York City on Dec. 12, 1745. In 1764 he graduated from King's College (now Columbia University). He became a lawyer in 1768 and soon became one of the most respected men in his profession in the colonies.

When the American Revolution began, Jay was made a member of the New York Committee of Correspondence, the Continental Congress, and the New York Provincial Congress. He helped draft a

John Jay (top left), *along with other chief justices, including* (left to right, top to bottom) *John Rutledge, Oliver Ellsworth, John Marshall, Roger B. Taney, Salmon P. Chase, Morrison R. Waite, and Melville W. Fuller.* Library of Congress, Washington, D.C. (neg. no. LC-USZ62-17681)

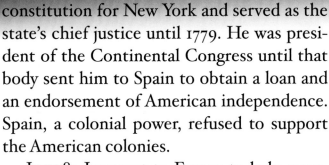

constitution for New York and served as the state's chief justice until 1779. He was president of the Continental Congress until that body sent him to Spain to obtain a loan and an endorsement of American independence. Spain, a colonial power, refused to support the American colonies.

In 1782 Jay went to France to help negotiate a peace treaty with Great Britain. He returned home in 1784 to find that Congress had named him secretary of foreign affairs. Jay later helped win ratification of the new federal Constitution by collaborating with Alexander Hamilton and James Madison to write *The Federalist Papers*.

When a new government was formed under the Constitution, Jay became the first chief justice of the United States, in which capacity he was instrumental in shaping Supreme Court procedures in its formative years. In 1794 he was sent to London to settle many problems remaining from the Revolution. An agreement, known as the Jay Treaty, was drawn up. It provided that the British would withdraw from areas they still held in the Northwest Territory and that the United States would pay debts contracted by its citizens before the Revolution. It also established joint commissions to settle disputed parts of the boundary between the United States and Canada. Thomas Jefferson and others assailed Jay for having failed to secure Britain's promise to stop interfering with U.S. ships at sea.

In Jay's absence he was elected governor of New York. He served two terms (1795–1801) then retired to his estate near Bedford, N.Y., where he died on May 17, 1829.

The Father of the Constitution, James Madison was the fourth president of the United States, serving from 1809 to 1817. Succeeding Thomas Jefferson as president, Madison was confronted with British naval threats overseas and hostile Native Americans stirred by British resentment of the United States. These factors contributed to the War of 1812 against Great Britain.

Madison was born on March 16, 1751, in Port Conway, Va. His parents were James Madison, Sr., a prominent landowner, and Eleanor Conway. Madison lived most of his life at Montpelier, his family's plantation. After graduating from the College of New Jersey (now Princeton University) in 1771, Madison returned to Montpelier and served in the Virginia legislature. In 1776 he worked alongside Thomas Jefferson in writing Virginia's constitution, a set of laws that became the model for the U.S. Constitution. In 1779 he was elected to the Continental Congress, where he served until the end of the American Revolution.

At the Constitutional Convention of 1787, Madison outlined the Virginia Plan, a set of 15 resolutions designed to establish a national government. The federal government would include three branches—a national legislature to enact laws, an executive leader to govern the nation, and a national judiciary composed of the courts—with elected representatives in each branch holding office for designated terms. Madison drafted a large portion of the Constitution based on principles of a strong national government and an even distribution of authority within its branches. His dedication to these values and his diligent participation in the convention earned him the title Father of the Constitution.

To promote the Constitution's ratification, Madison collaborated with Alexander Hamilton and John Jay to write *The Federalist Papers*, a series of essays on the Constitution and republican government published in newspapers in 1787–88. Madison's essays in *The Federalist Papers* proclaimed that stability, liberty, and justice in the country could be achieved most effectively by the decisions of a majority rule formed by compromise and conciliation. On Sept. 17, 1787, a total of 39

delegates signed the Constitution, including Madison, Hamilton, and George Washington, who presided over the convention.

In 1789 Madison was elected to the new House of Representatives. There he helped pass the Bill of Rights, the first 10 amendments to the Constitution. During his time in Congress, Madison came to believe that the federal government should not have more power than the states. He shared that opinion with his friend Thomas Jefferson.

In 1794 Madison was introduced to a young widow named Dolley Payne Todd. Dolley had one surviving child, John Payne Todd, from her previous marriage. The couple married on Sept. 15, 1794. They raised John Todd, but never had any children together.

From 1801 to 1809 Madison served under President Jefferson as secretary of state. Elected president in 1808, Madison took office in March 1809 on the heels of an unstable national economy and naval threats from both Britain and France. Believing that Britain was bent on permanent suppression of American overseas commerce, Madison forbade trade with Britain in 1810 and signed a declaration of war in 1812.

As commander-in-chief during the War of 1812, Madison was unable to convince Congress to increase funds to support the military. As a result, the United States lacked the trained troops and munitions necessary for launching a successful war campaign. U.S. achievements in the war were limited to a few successful ground assaults and strategic naval battles.

Madison planned offensives into Canada and commissioned American Revolution veteran General William Hull to lead the U.S. attacks. Hull's tactics were poorly organized, and he was forced to retreat to Detroit where he surrendered to British troops and their Native American allies in August 1812. Further attempts to invade Canada were equally disastrous.

Amid the series of defeats on the battlefield came the presidential election of 1812, and New England Federalists labeled Madison as an incompetent leader during his campaign. His opponents used their antiwar rhetoric to promote their candidate, DeWitt Clinton of New York. Nevertheless, Madison had little difficulty in securing a second term.

The United States fared much better in its naval campaigns. The frigates *Constitution*

and *United States* won decisive encounters against British warships in 1812. In the Battle of Lake Erie U.S. naval Capt. Oliver H. Perry took control of Lake Erie in an engagement over a British fleet in September 1813. This victory helped ensure U.S. control of the Northwest.

Madison had named General William Henry Harrison as the commander of U.S. forces in the Northwest after Hull's surrender at Detroit. Harrison drove the British from Detroit, and on Oct. 5, 1813, defeated the British army and their Native Americans at the Battle of the Thames in Ontario, Canada. The Shawnee chief, Tecumseh, was killed in this battle, and thereafter the Native Americans loyal to Great Britain broke their alliance.

In August 1814 British troops marched into Washington, D.C., and burned the Executive Mansion, the Capitol, and several other government buildings. Madison and his Cabinet retreated to Virginia during the attack. Neither the United States nor Great Britain gained any significant military or territorial advantages as a result of the war, however. The Treaty of Ghent was signed on

Dec. 24, 1814, in Belgium, officially ending the conflict.

Among other notable events during Madison's presidency was the congressional charter for the second Bank of the United States in 1816. After the inauguration of James Monroe as president in 1817, Madison returned to Montpelier, where he spent the next 19 years managing his 5,000-acre (2,000-hectare) farm. He died on June 28, 1836.

CHAPTER 6

ALEXANDER HAMILTON

One of the youngest and brightest of the founders of the United States, Alexander Hamilton favored strong central government. As the nation's first secretary of the treasury he established responsible financial policies that helped the country prosper.

Hamilton was born on the island of Nevis, in the British West Indies, of Scottish and French descent. He was born on January 11, probably in 1755. (For years his birth year was given as 1757, but research now indicates he was probably born two years earlier.) When he was about 15 he was sent to school in New York City, and was studying at King's College (now Columbia University) when the American Revolution began. He enlisted in a New York artillery company and soon became a captain. He was introduced to the American commander-in-chief, George Washington, who liked the young officer. From 1777 to 1781, Hamilton served on Washington's staff with the rank of lieutenant colonel.

During the war Hamilton decided that the new nation would need a strong central

Portrait of Alexander Hamilton, by John Trumbull. SuperStock/
Getty Images

government. In the critical period after the
war, he advocated writing a new constitution
to replace the weak Articles of Confederation.
He persuaded New York to send delegates

to the Philadelphia Convention, and was one of the three chosen. The other two were bitter anti-Federalists who, until they withdrew from the convention, constantly outvoted him. Hamilton signed the Constitution for New York.

Hamilton believed a limited monarchy like that of Britain to be the best form of government. Failing that, he would have preferred a strong aristocratic republic, with members of the government elected for life. Nevertheless, he exerted his great influence in support of the new Constitution. With James Madison and John Jay he wrote a series of essays in its defense. They were signed "The Federalist." These essays, collectively called *The Federalist Papers*, not only helped win New York's ratification, but also had a tremendous influence throughout the country. Written to serve a particular purpose in Hamilton's time, they continue to be of great value to students of law and political science. *The Federalist Papers* are regarded today as classic commentaries on the Constitution.

Washington chose Hamilton to be the first secretary of the treasury. It was in this office that he did most to shape the struggling young government. Hamilton's interpretations of the direct and implied powers of the Constitution later influenced the thinking of John Marshall, the fourth chief justice of the United States.

Hamilton's financial measures assured payment of the foreign and domestic debts of the United States. Under his leadership the federal government also took over the debts contracted by the separate states as a result of the Revolution. Hamilton gained congressional support for this provision by agreeing to locate the federal capital on the Potomac River. Hamilton restored the credit of the United States—perhaps his greatest achievement—and also established a national bank.

Thomas Jefferson, Washington's secretary of state, opposed Hamilton's efforts to strengthen the federal government. Jefferson was a firm believer in states' rights. In foreign affairs Hamilton was pro-British. Jefferson favored revolutionary France. These two men became the leaders of the first organized political parties in the United States, the Federalists and the Democratic-Republicans.

Jefferson resigned from Washington's cabinet in 1793 and Hamilton left in 1795, but their political feud continued. John Adams was elected president in 1796. In the election of 1800, Jefferson ran against him, with Aaron Burr as Jefferson's vice presidential running mate. Jefferson and Burr won, but the two received an equal number of electoral votes. Under the electoral procedures of the time, the electors had cast their votes for the pair without indicating which should be president and which vice president. The House of Representatives had to break the tie.

An illustration shows the fatal shot, fired by Aaron Burr, that killed Alexander Hamilton during their 1804 duel in Weehawken, N.J. Kean Collection/Archive Photos/Getty Images

Hamilton distrusted Burr. He also knew that the voters wanted Jefferson to be president. Therefore, he temporarily abandoned his feud with Jefferson and swung the Federalist majority in Jefferson's favor. Then, in 1804, Hamilton further alienated Burr by using his influence to prevent Burr from being elected governor of New York.

Infuriated, Burr challenged Hamilton to a duel. Hamilton reluctantly accepted. Early in the morning of July 11, 1804, Hamilton and Burr faced each other at Weehawken on the New Jersey shore of the Hudson River, opposite New York City. The first shot mortally wounded Hamilton, and he died the next day.

The fourth chief justice of the U.S. Supreme Court was John Marshall, who proved to be one of the most influential jurists in American history. Marshall believed that the United States should develop a strong federal government, and he interpreted the Constitution in such a way as to expand the role of the Court.

John Marshall was born on Sept. 24, 1755, in a log cabin near Germantown (now Midland), Va. The first of 15 children, he had little formal education. At the age of 20 he enlisted in the Continental Army, in which he rose to the rank of captain. After the American Revolution, he briefly studied law.

Marshall was elected to the Virginia legislature, where he served for eight sessions. In the Virginia convention of 1788, he and James Madison won the battle for ratification of the federal Constitution, defeating the opposition of Patrick Henry and Richard Henry Lee. President George Washington offered Marshall the post of attorney general, then that of minister to France. Marshall declined both. He did accept an appointment from President John Adams to be one of three commissioners

sent to France in 1797–98. A term in Congress followed, and then a year as secretary of state in Adams' cabinet. Adams nominated him as chief justice of the Supreme Court, and the nomination was confirmed on Jan. 27, 1801.

His first great case, that of *Marbury vs. Madison*, was in 1803. In his ruling on that case Marshall declared that it was the duty of the Court to disregard any act of Congress—and hence of a state legislature—that it thought contrary to the federal Constitution. On this fundamental decision rests the chief power exercised by the Supreme Court today, that of judicial review.

Equally far-reaching was the Court's decision in the case of *McCulloch vs. Maryland* (1819). This decision affirmed the Hamiltonian idea of implied powers of the government—that is, that Congress has not only the powers explicitly granted to it by the Constitution but also all authority "appropriate" to carry out such powers. The Court's decision also established that the United States is a nation, with the powers appropriate to a nation, and not merely a weak confederation.

Marshall served as chief justice for the rest of his life, participating in more than 1,000 Court decisions. He died on July 6, 1835, in Philadelphia, Pa.

The fifth president of the United States was James Monroe, whose most celebrated achievement during his administration (1817–25) was the proposal of the Monroe Doctrine in 1823. It was a basic policy for the defense of North and South America against foreign intrusion.

Monroe was born on April 28, 1758, in Westmoreland County, Va. His family lived on a modest 600-acre (240-hectare) estate. When his father died in 1774, James became proprietor of the estate. In the same year he enrolled at the College of William and Mary in Williamsburg, Va., but he left in 1776 to fight in the American Revolution.

After the war Monroe studied law under Thomas Jefferson. Monroe was elected to the Virginia legislature in 1782. From 1783 to 1786 he served in the Continental Congress, during which time he met the socially prominent Elizabeth Kortright, whose father was a former British officer and New York merchant. They were married on Feb. 16, 1786, in New York City. The couple had three children.

In 1790 Monroe was elected to the U.S. Senate, where he vigorously opposed the Federalist-controlled government of President George Washington. Nevertheless, in 1794 Washington appointed Monroe as U.S. minister to France. Eventually Washington concluded that Monroe could not represent his government properly and recalled him late in 1796.

Monroe still held the confidence of the Virginia voters, who elected him governor in 1799. When Jefferson became president, he sent Monroe to France to help buy the Louisiana Territory. Upon completing his duties in France, Monroe was named U.S. minister to Great Britain.

Monroe returned to the United States in 1807. He was elected to the Virginia legislature in 1810 and became governor again in 1811. In November of that year he resigned to become secretary of state under President James Madison. In this office he had to confront the ongoing crisis with Great Britain, as the British navy persisted in harassing U.S. ships. Madison and Monroe accepted that war was the only solution, and in 1812 Congress declared war on Great Britain. The War of 1812 continued through 1814. In the

latter part of the war Monroe served as secretary of war in addition to secretary of state.

In 1816 Monroe was elected president
as the Democratic-Republican candidate,

Portrait of U.S. President James Monroe. **Buyenlarge/Archive Photos/
Getty Images**

defeating the Federalist candidate Rufus King. Monroe took office on March 4, 1817, with Daniel D. Tompkins, former governor of New York, as vice president. He was reelected in 1820.

Monroe faced the country's first conflict over slavery after the territory of Missouri applied for statehood in 1817. Missouri wanted no restrictions on slavery, but Northern congressmen tried to limit the practice. Representatives from the Southern states were outraged. Amid a fierce debate over slavery and the government's right to restrict it, Congress adjourned without resolving the Missouri question.

Although a slave owner, Monroe was a member of the American Colonization Society, which tried unsuccessfully to free the slaves and resettle them in Africa. Nevertheless, Monroe refused to support banning slavery in Missouri because the U.S. Constitution included a slavery provision for new states entering the Union.

After Maine applied for statehood in 1819 as a free state, the North and the South compromised under the direction of Speaker of the House Henry Clay. Maine would enter the United States as a free state and Missouri as a slave state, but slavery was banned from then on in territories north of Missouri's southern border. Maine was admitted as the 23rd state in 1820, and Missouri was admitted as the 24th state in 1821. Though the Missouri Compromise ended the crisis peacefully, it marked the beginning of the prolonged conflict over slavery that led to the American Civil War.

Monroe gained the territory of Florida from Spain in 1821. In 1823 he made a lasting contribution to U.S. foreign policy with a statement to Congress. The statement, which in the 1850s became known as the Monroe Doctrine, came in response to the threat that European powers would help Spain reclaim its recently lost colonies in North and South America.

The Monroe Doctrine made four basic points: The United States would not interfere in the political affairs of Europe; the United States recognized and would not interfere with existing colonies in Latin America; the Western Hemisphere was closed to future colonization; and any attempt by a European country to oppress or control any country in the Americas would be considered a hostile act against the United States. As the United States grew into a world power, future presidents, such as James K. Polk and Theodore Roosevelt, upheld and expanded on Monroe's principles.

After his second term ended in 1825, Monroe retired to his plantation at Oak Hill, Va. He later moved to New York City, where he died on July 4, 1831.

The eldest son of John Adams, John Quincy Adams followed in his father's footsteps to serve as president of the United States, from 1825 to 1829. As the sixth U.S. president, the younger Adams achieved very few of his plans for improvements within the country. From the outset of his presidency, he faced unmerciful scrutiny from his political adversary, Andrew Jackson, and the biting criticism of Jackson's followers.

John Quincy Adams was born on July 11, 1767, in Braintree (now Quincy), Mass. He grew up amid the colonial uprisings leading to the American Revolution. After accompanying his father to Europe on several diplomatic missions, he returned to Massachusetts and entered Harvard College (now Harvard University). He graduated in 1787 and became a lawyer in Boston. He was later appointed U.S. minister to the Netherlands (1794) and to Prussia (1797).

Adams married Louisa Catherine Johnson on July 26, 1797. He had met her in France during one of his father's diplomatic assignments. Born in London, Louisa was the daughter of Joshua Johnson, a U.S. consul in Great Britain. The couple had three sons.

In 1802 Adams was elected to the Massachusetts Senate, and the following year won election to the U.S. Senate. In 1809 President James Madison sent Adams to St. Petersburg as U.S. minister to Russia. Adams witnessed the disaster that befell Napoleon I's French army as it invaded Russia in 1812. Adams was still in St. Petersburg when the War of 1812 broke out between the United States and Great Britain. In 1814 he led a delegation to Belgium to negotiate the Treaty of Ghent, which ended the war. For the next two years Adams worked in London as U.S. minister to Great Britain.

Adams returned to the United States in 1817 and became secretary of state under President James Monroe. In that role Adams helped persuade Spain to give control of Florida to the United States. He also helped create the Monroe Doctrine, a warning to European countries not to extend their power in the Western Hemisphere.

As President Monroe's second term came to a close in 1824, four candidates vied to replace him: Adams, Treasury Secretary William H.

Crawford, Speaker of the House Henry Clay, and General Andrew Jackson. Jackson won the popular vote, but none of the candidates received a necessary majority of electoral votes. Jackson finished with 99, Adams with 84, Crawford with 41, and Clay with 37. The decision was then turned over to the House of Representatives. Clay was dropped from consideration because the House could select from only the top three candidates. Clay endorsed Adams, giving Adams the votes he needed for victory. Upon his election, Adams appointed Clay secretary of state.

Jackson and his followers were outraged over what they called a "corrupt bargain." Jackson felt deprived of the presidency after winning the popular vote, and he believed that Clay had thrown his support behind Adams in exchange for a cabinet appointment. Jackson's supporters, called Jacksonians, were determined to undermine the Adams administration at every turn.

Adams was inaugurated on March 4, 1825. He outlined a forward-thinking agenda for his presidency. He supported the gradual development of Western territories, and petitioned Congress for federal aid to build more roads and canals. To strengthen higher

Lithograph of a daguerreotype image of the sixth U.S. president—and son of the second president—John Quincy Adams. Library of Congress/Archive Photos/Getty Images

education and stimulate science, he proposed creating a national university, a naval academy, and national astronomical observatories. However, the Jacksonians in Congress rejected his plans.

Adams faced further hostility in 1828 when he proposed a high tariff on imported industrial goods. The tariff was intended to protect New England factories from European competitors. Southerners opposed the tariff, believing that it would harm their economy. The Jacksonians in Congress tried to defeat the tariff, but it was approved nevertheless. Southerners called it the Tariff of Abominations. The unpopularity of the tariff helped to propel Jackson to victory over Adams in the 1828 presidential election.

Adams returned to his home in Braintree in 1829, but his retirement was brief. In 1830 Massachusetts elected him to the U.S. House of Representatives, where he served for the remainder of his life. In Congress Adams argued against the expansion of slavery. He also oversaw the establishment of the Smithsonian Institute in Washington, D.C. On Feb. 21, 1848, while speaking on the floor of the House, Adams suffered a stroke and collapsed. He died two days later.

A military hero with a humble political background, Andrew Jackson became the seventh president of the United States in 1829. His election is commonly regarded as a turning point in U.S. history. Jackson was the first president from west of the Appalachian Mountains and the first to be elected through a direct appeal to the people rather than through the backing of an established political organization. The Democratic Party, developed in the 1830s, is a legacy of his presidency.

Andrew Jackson was born on March 15, 1767, in the western Carolinas, probably in what is now South Carolina. Andrew's father died a few weeks before the boy's birth, leaving his mother to raise three sons on her own. The area offered little opportunity for formal education, and what little schooling Andrew received was interrupted by the American Revolution.

Andrew joined the colonial militia and fought in several backwoods skirmishes against the British. In 1781 he was captured by British soldiers. When a British officer commanded him to clean his boots, the boy refused and was struck across the face with a saber. His mother and two brothers died

Former military commander Andrew Jackson, the first U.S. president elected without the backing of an organized political party. After his election, his supporters formed what became known as the Democratic Party. **FPG/Taxi/Getty Images**

during the closing years of the war, direct or indirect casualties of the war. These tragic experiences fixed in Jackson's mind a lifelong hostility toward Great Britain.

After the end of Revolution, Jackson studied law at an office in Salisbury, North Carolina, and, from 1788, worked as a lawyer in a western region that later became Tennessee. Jackson married Rachel Donelson Robards in 1791. They later adopted Robards' nephew and named him Andrew Jackson, Jr.

In 1796 Jackson helped write the constitution for the new state of Tennessee. The state's voters elected him as their first representative to the U.S. House of Representatives. In 1797–98 he served as a U.S. senator. Jackson then became a judge for the highest court in Tennessee.

In 1802 Jackson was made a major general in the Tennessee militia. When war broke out between the United States and Great Britain in 1812, Jackson offered the services of his militia to the United States. Sent to the Alabama-Georgia region to fight the Creek Indians, who were allied with the British, Jackson and his militia crushed the Creek at the battle of Horseshoe Bend in 1814. The Creek campaign was typical of Jackson as a

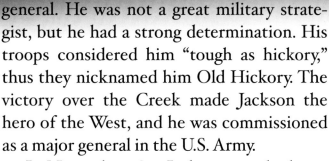

general. He was not a great military strategist, but he had a strong determination. His troops considered him "tough as hickory," thus they nicknamed him Old Hickory. The victory over the Creek made Jackson the hero of the West, and he was commissioned as a major general in the U.S. Army.

In November 1814 Jackson marched into Spanish-held Florida and captured Pensacola, preparing for the U.S. occupation of Florida. Prior to Jackson's arrival, the British army had evacuated the city and advanced by sea to Louisiana. Jackson marched his army overland to New Orleans. A series of small skirmishes culminated in the Battle of New Orleans on Jan. 8, 1815. Jackson's forces decisively defeated the British army and forced it to withdraw. The victory did not affect the outcome of the war as, unknown to Jackson, a peace treaty had already been signed. Nevertheless, it raised the country's morale and made Jackson a national hero.

In 1817 Jackson was again sent to the Alabama-Georgia region, this time to defend U.S. settlers against attacks by Seminole Indians from Florida. Without awaiting orders, Jackson marched into Spanish-held Florida, burned Seminole villages, and captured Pensacola and St. Marks in what became known as the First Seminole War. These actions brought sharp protest from Spain, as well as harsh criticism in Congress, but Secretary of State John Quincy Adams defended Jackson and defused the crisis. Spain ceded Florida to the United States in 1821.

In 1823 Jackson returned to the Senate. The next year he ran against three other candidates for president. Jackson won the highest number of votes but not an electoral majority. The decision went to the House of Representatives, which chose John Quincy Adams. Jackson ran for the presidency again in 1828. His war record and humble background attracted voters. They saw him as a man of the people, not a rich politician from the East. With the support of the western states, Jackson defeated President Adams. Jackson's supporters formed the new Democratic Party, which helped him win a second term in 1832.

Upon taking office as president, Jackson replaced many federal officials with his political supporters, a practice that became known as the spoils system. His administration acquiesced in the illegal seizure of

Cherokee land in Georgia and later forcibly expelled about 15,000 Cherokee who refused to leave. Their march west in the fall and winter of 1838–39, during which nearly a quarter of the Cherokee died of starvation, illness, and exposure, became known as the Trail of Tears.

When South Carolina claimed the right to nullify a federally imposed tariff, Jackson asked for and received congressional authority to use the military to enforce federal laws in the state. His reelection in 1832 was partially the result of his controversial veto of a bill to recharter the Bank of the United States, which was unpopular with many. The intensity of the political struggles during Jackson's tenure led to the strengthening of the Democratic Party and the further development of the two-party system.

In 1837 Jackson retired to his home, the Hermitage, near Nashville, Tenn. His wife had died after his election in 1828. Jackson's health grew worse until he died at home on June 8, 1845.

The most dramatic of the Indians' struggles to hold their lands against the white man was the one led by the great Shawnee chief Tecumseh. He was born on Mad River, near the present-day city of Springfield, Ohio, in about 1768. From his earliest childhood he saw suffering brought to his people by the whites.

In 1808 Tecumseh and his brother Tenskwatawa, a religious leader called the Prophet, established a village in northern Indiana. They persuaded the Indians there to avoid liquor, to cultivate their land, and to return to traditional Indian ways of life. The village came to be known as Prophet's Town.

Meanwhile Tecumseh was forming a defensive confederacy of Indian tribes, traveling throughout the East and Midwest. "Our fathers," he said to the Indians, "from their tombs, reproach us as slaves and cowards." He won the allegiance of many tribes.

At that time William Henry Harrison was governor of the Indiana Territory. He induced a number of individual tribes to

Shawnee Indian chief Tecumseh, who led a confederacy of Native American tribes in a resistance movement against the encroachment of white settlers on Indian land. **Hulton Archive/Getty Images**

give up great areas in the region that is now Indiana and Illinois. At a council in Vincennes in 1810, Tecumseh demanded that land be returned to the Indians. Since it belonged to all of them, he argued, individual chiefs did not have the right to barter it away. His demand was rejected. He then traveled to Canada to consult the British and, afterward, to the Southwest to enlist support of Indian tribes there.

Governor Harrison undertook an expedition against Prophet's Town during Tecumseh's absence, in September 1811. On November 7, after a fierce battle, he destroyed the village. This defeat scattered the Indian warriors. When the War of 1812 broke out, Tecumseh joined the British as a brigadier general. He was killed at the battle of the Thames in Ontario on Oct. 5, 1813. He is buried on Walpole Island, Ont.

Native American scholar Sequoyah was the creator of the writing system used by the Cherokee. The sequoia tree was named in his honor.

Sequoyah was born in about 1770 in Taskigi (now in Tennessee). He was probably the son of a British trader named Nathaniel Gist. Sequoyah was raised by his Cherokee mother and became a talented artist. From 1813 to 1814 he fought for the U.S. Army in the Creek War, a conflict between the U.S. government and Native Americans called the Creek.

Sequoyah believed that white people had superior power because of their written language, which allowed them to have a great deal of knowledge. About 1809 Sequoyah began to develop a system of writing for the Cherokee, believing that their own increased knowledge would help them maintain their independence from the white people. He adapted letters from English, Greek, and Hebrew that represented the syllables of the spoken Cherokee language. By 1821 he had created a system of 86 symbols.

Sequoyah taught his daughter and other young people of the tribe to write. The simplicity of his system enabled pupils to learn it rapidly. Soon Cherokees throughout the nation were teaching it in their schools and publishing books and newspapers in their own Cherokee language. Sequoyah died in August 1843, near San Fernando, Mexico.

U.S. President Thomas Jefferson was interested in knowing more about the country west of the Mississippi and finding a water route to the Pacific Ocean. He also wanted to make diplomatic contact with Indian groups in the area and expand the fur trade. In 1803, two years after he became president, he asked Congress for $2,500 for an expedition. To head the expedition, Jefferson chose his young secretary, Capt. Meriwether Lewis. Lewis invited his friend Lieut. William Clark to share the leadership. Though Lewis was chief in command, Clark had more frontier experience. More than once he saved the party from disaster.

William Clark was born in Caroline County, Va., on Aug. 1, 1770. He was still a child when an elder brother, George Rogers Clark, won the Old Northwest for the United States. When William was 14 the family moved to Louisville, Ky. As a youth William helped defend the pioneer settlements against Indians. In 1792 he was commissioned a lieutenant under General Anthony

William Clark, portrait by Charles Willson Peale, 1810; in Independence National Historical Park, Philadelphia. Courtesy of the Independence National Historical Park Collection, Philadelphia

Wayne. Meriwether Lewis served in the same division.

In 1803, after he had accepted Lewis' invitation to help lead an expedition to the Pacific Northwest, Clark recruited men in Kentucky to join the Corps of Discovery and oversaw the group's training at Camp River Dubois in Illinois. The group set out on their expedition from St. Louis, Mo., on May 14, 1804, with Clark operating as the party's principal waterman and cartographer.

Clark was often more skillful than Lewis at Indian negotiations. Consequently, the expedition's Shoshone interpreter, Sacagawea, and her family spent the majority of their time with Clark.

After the party returned to St. Louis, Clark made his home there. In 1813 he became governor of the Missouri Territory. Clark remarried when his first wife died in 1820. He died on Sept. 1, 1838.

The name of Meriwether Lewis is closely linked with that of fellow American explorer William Clark. Together they led the Lewis and Clark Expedition of 1804–06.

Lewis was born on Aug. 18, 1774, on a plantation near Charlottesville, Va. Thomas Jefferson, a neighbor, was a friend of the family. Lewis studied with private tutors, hunted, and learned nature lore. In 1794 he served in the militia during the Whiskey Rebellion. The next year he fought against Native Americans in the Northwest Territory. Between campaigns he lived in the wilderness and learned Native American languages and customs.

Soon after Jefferson became U.S. president, Lewis became his private secretary. They often discussed the exploration of a land route to the Pacific Ocean. Lewis was eager to lead the expedition. Congress, at Jefferson's request, appropriated $2,500, the sum Lewis estimated was needed. Jefferson asked Lewis to choose a companion officer, and Lewis selected Clark. The success of the

Meriwether Lewis, portrait by Charles Willson Peale; in Independence National Historical Park, Philadelphia. **Courtesy of the Independence National Historical Park Collection, Philadelphia**

expedition was due to the combined abilities of the two leaders.

In 1807, following the completion of the expedition, Jefferson appointed Lewis governor of the Louisiana Territory, with headquarters in St. Louis. Lewis' service in his new position was brief. In 1809 he started on a trip to Washington, D.C. On October 11 he was found shot to death at an inn near what is now Hohenwald, Tenn. Some historians believe that he killed himself, while others contend that he was murdered.

A Native American teenager named Sacagawea served as an interpreter for the Lewis and Clark Expedition to the western United States. A Lemhi Shoshone Indian, she traveled thousands of miles through the wilderness with the explorers. Many memorials have been raised in her honor, in part for the fortitude with which she faced hardship on the difficult journey.

Sacagawea is thought to have been born in about 1788, near the Continental Divide at what is now the Idaho-Montana border. In about 1800, when she was about 12 years old, a raiding party of Hidatsa Indians captured her near the headwaters of the Missouri River. The Hidatsa made her a slave and took her to the Mandan-Hidatsa villages near what is now Bismarck, N.D. In about 1804 she became one of the wives of the French Canadian fur trader Toussaint Charbonneau. (Sacagawea may have been sold to him.)

The explorers Meriwether Lewis and William Clark arrived at the Mandan-Hidatsa villages and built a fort there in

Statue of Sacagawea, shown carrying her son on the journey west with Lewis and Clark, in Bismark, N.D. Visions of America/Joe Sohm/Photodisc/Getty Images

which to spend the winter. They hired Charbonneau as an interpreter to help them speak with the various Indian natives they would encounter on their expedition. However, he did not speak Shoshone. The expedition would need to communicate with the Shoshone to acquire horses to use to cross the mountains. For this reason, the explorers agreed that the pregnant Sacagawea should also accompany them. On Feb. 11, 1805, she gave birth to a son, Jean Baptiste. Sacagawea took her infant along on the expedition, which helped allay the suspicions of approaching Indian tribes—a woman and child accompanying a party of men indicated peaceful intentions.

By mid-August the expedition encountered a band of Shoshone. Their leader was Sacagawea's brother, Cameahwait. The reunion of Sacagawea and her brother helped Lewis and Clark obtain the horses and guide that enabled them to cross the Rocky Mountains.

Sacagawea was not the guide for the expedition, as some have wrongly portrayed her. She did, however, recognize landmarks in southwestern Montana. She also informed

Clark that Bozeman Pass was the best route between the Missouri and Yellowstone rivers on their return journey. Sacagawea and her family left the expedition when they arrived back at the Mandan-Hidatsa villages.

It is believed that Sacagawea died shortly after giving birth to a daughter, Lisette, on Dec. 20, 1812, at Fort Manuel, near what is now Mobridge, S.D. Clark became the legal guardian of her two children.

For 40 years Henry Clay exercised leadership in the politics of the United States that has seldom been equaled. He was a charming man, powerful speaker, and brilliant statesman. Nevertheless, he repeatedly failed to gain the presidency. Clay was the author of the famous saying, "I would rather be right than be president."

Clay was born on April 12, 1777, in Hanover County, Va. Encouraged by his stepfather, Clay studied law under the prominent professor George Wythe, and was admitted to the Virginia bar when he was 20. Shortly afterward he moved to Kentucky. There his great leadership and eloquence soon won for him a place in the Kentucky legislature.

Two years later, in 1806, Clay was chosen to fill an unexpired term in the U.S. Senate. Although he had not yet reached the legal age of 30, he was permitted to take his seat and at once became prominent. In 1811 he was elected to Congress, and on the first day of the session was chosen Speaker of the House. With the exception of one term, which he refused (1821–23), he remained a representative and the Speaker of the House until 1825. In addition to these 12 years in the House, he served for almost 20 years in the Senate.

At the beginning of his career, Clay won popularity throughout the country by boldly urging war with Great Britain. John C. Calhoun ably supported him. The two "war hawks," as they were called, persuaded a reluctant Congress and president to a declaration of hostilities against Great Britain in 1812. Clay was chosen one of the commissioners who arranged the Treaty of Ghent, which ended the War of 1812.

Clay was one of four candidates in the presidential election of 1824, none of whom received a majority of votes. In such an emergency the choice of president rests with the House of Representatives. Clay stood fourth on the list and, in accordance with the Constitution, was dropped from the list of candidates. William Crawford, another candidate, suffered a stroke. The choice therefore lay between John Quincy Adams and Andrew Jackson, the two remaining candidates. Clay used his influence in favor of Adams, who was elected. When Adams appointed Clay to be his secretary of state,

the charge of "bargain and corruption" was at once raised by Jackson's friends. The bargain charge, in spite of its injustice, followed Clay to the grave. In 1832 and again in 1844, Clay was again a candidate for the presidency but was defeated, first by Andrew Jackson and then by James K. Polk.

Clay declared "the leading and paramount object" of his public life to be the

Portrait of statesman Henry Clay. SuperStock/Getty Images

preservation of the Union. For finding solutions to numerous controversies between the North and South he earned the title the Great Pacificator. In one of his speeches, in 1848, he said, "I know no South, no North, no East, no West, to which I owe any allegiance."

Three times Clay was able by his compromises to bring about concessions that, though satisfying neither North nor South, delayed the inevitable struggle that was to become the American Civil War. In 1820, while still Speaker of the House of Representatives, he played an important part in the Missouri Compromise. In 1833, when South Carolina attempted to nullify a tariff and threatened to secede from the Union, Clay stepped into the breach with the compromise Tariff of 1833. In 1850, at the most severe crisis the country had yet faced, he again came forward as the author of the Compromise of 1850, a series of measures that, in part, admitted California as a free state but left the question of slavery in the new territories of New Mexico and Utah to be settled by the local residents. The Compromise of 1850 has been credited with delaying the American Civil War for a decade.

Clay died in Washington, D.C., on June 29, 1852.

CHAPTER 17

FRANCIS SCOTT KEY

A lawyer who wrote verse as a hobby, Francis Scott Key penned the words that became "The Star-Spangled Banner" after a battle in the War of 1812. The words were sung to the tune of the English drinking song "To Anacreon in Heaven."

Lawyer turned lyricist Francis Scott Key. **FPG/Archive Photos/ Getty Images**

Francis Scott Key was born on Terra Rubra, his family's estate in western Maryland, on Aug. 1, 1779. Until he was 10 he was educated at home. After attending preparatory school at Annapolis, he entered St. John's College and then prepared for a legal career in the office of Judge Jeremiah Chase. Key opened a successful law practice in Georgetown (now part of Washington, D.C.).

After the burning of Washington by the British in the War of 1812, Key was sent to the British fleet anchored in Chesapeake Bay to secure the release of a friend. He was detained

Visitors walk past the flag that inspired Francis Scott Key to write "The Star-Spangled Banner," on display at the Smithsonian Institution in August 2010. **Tim Sloan/AFP/Getty Images**

aboard ship overnight on Sept. 13, 1814, during the bombardment of Fort McHenry. When he saw the U.S. flag still flying over the fortress the next morning, he wrote the words to what was later called "The Star-Spangled Banner" but was first printed under the title "Defence of Fort M'Henry". The song quickly became popular and was adopted by the army and navy as the national anthem, but it was not until 1931 that it became officially recognized as such by an act of Congress.

Key went on to serve as attorney for the District of Columbia from 1833. He died in Baltimore, Md., on Jan. 11, 1843.

An influential Southern statesman, John C. Calhoun was a fervent supporter of states' rights and the expansion of slavery. Calhoun served as a member of the U.S. House of Representatives at the time of the War of 1812 and later as secretary of war, vice president, secretary of state, and senator from South Carolina.

John Caldwell Calhoun was born on March 18, 1782, on a frontier farm in Abbeville County, S.C. In 1804 he graduated from Yale College in New Haven, Conn., with highest honors and began studying law. He was admitted to the bar in 1807 and practiced law in Abbeville for several years. In 1811 he married a cousin, Floride Bonneau Calhoun.

After a brief term in South Carolina's legislature, Calhoun was elected to the House of Representatives in 1811. Along with Henry Clay he became a leader of the war hawks, who successfully pressed for war with Great Britain. After the war he continued to promote the widespread authority of the federal government. He also endorsed a protective

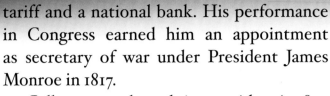

tariff and a national bank. His performance in Congress earned him an appointment as secretary of war under President James Monroe in 1817.

Calhoun was elected vice president in 1824 under John Quincy Adams and was reelected in 1828 under Andrew Jackson. During this time a change took place in his ideals. The ardent nationalist became a steadfast champion of states' rights. He led the opposition to an 1828 tariff that Southerners claimed they were being forced to pay for the benefit of New England manufacturers. Calhoun stated that the tariff was unconstitutional and argued that a state had the constitutional right to declare a federal law null and void within its limits.

When South Carolina tried to put Calhoun's idea of nullification into practice late in 1832, President Jackson warned the state not to overstep its boundaries. Subsequently, Calhoun resigned as vice president and entered the Senate to lead the fight against the president's policies. Thereafter, Calhoun and Jackson were bitter political enemies.

For the last 20 years of his life Calhoun remained a tireless defender of the South and

States' rights supporter John C. Calhoun. MPI/Archive Photos/
Getty Images

of the institution of slavery. As secretary of state under President John Tyler (1844–45), Calhoun negotiated a treaty for the annexation of Texas, which extended slave territory in the United States. During the Senate debate on the Compromise of 1850 — a series of measures passed by the U.S. Congress in an effort to settle several outstanding slavery issues--he made his last public appearance. Calhoun was so ill that he had to be carried into the Senate chamber and so weak his speech had to be read for him. He died on March 31, 1850, in Washington, D.C.

CHAPTER 19

DANIEL WEBSTER

On Jan. 26 and 27, 1830, the U.S. Senate heard one of the greatest speeches ever delivered before it. Daniel Webster, senator from Massachusetts, delivered a speech that placed him in the front rank of American orators and won him enduring fame for statesmanship.

Webster was born on Jan. 18, 1782, in Salisbury, N.H. When he was 15 he entered Dartmouth College. After graduating from Dartmouth, he taught in an academy until he could send his brother Ezekiel to college. Webster was admitted to the Boston bar in 1805. At the age of 30 he was elected to the House of Representatives from New Hampshire. After remaining there for four years, he returned to the Boston bar.

In 1823 Webster was again in the House of Representatives, this time from Massachusetts. In 1827 the legislature of that state chose him to represent Massachusetts in the Senate. In January of 1830, Webster rose on the floor of the Senate in response to South Carolina Senator Robert Young Hayne's

Statesman and noted orator Daniel Webster. **Library of Congress Prints and Photographs Division**

rhetoric concerning the issue of nullification. Hayne, a confederate of John C. Calhoun, had said that the federal government was a mere confederation of states and that the states could refuse to obey any laws passed by Congress. Webster refuted Hayne's notion of "Liberty first and Union afterwards" with the memorable words, "Liberty and Union, now and forever, one and inseparable!"

An artist's vision of Daniel Webster giving his famous speech before Congress in 1830. **MPI/Archive Photos/Getty Images**

Webster remained in the Senate until his death in 1852, except while serving as secretary of state under presidents William Henry Harrison, John Tyler, and Millard Fillmore. While in this office he negotiated the Webster-Ashburton Treaty with Great Britain, signed in 1842, which settled the Maine boundary dispute.

Webster opposed the Mexican-American War (1846–48) and the adding of any more territory to the United States. After the war, however, he became involved in the sectional crisis concerning slavery in the new territories gained from Mexico. He supported Henry Clay's compromise proposals, one of which would organize new territories with no prohibition of slavery. (Webster argued that prohibition was unnecessary because the West was geographically unsuitable for plantation slavery.) For his support of compromise he was roundly condemned by antislavery factions.

While serving as secretary of state under Fillmore, Webster became so ill that he was forced to resign in 1852. He returned to his home in Marshfield, Mass., where he died on Oct. 24, 1852.

CHAPTER 20

Essayist, historian, and storyteller Washington Irving was the first of the great American writers. Before his time Europe had regarded American authors chiefly as curiosities. European critics were quick to recognize this new writer, however, so graceful was his style and so fascinating and delicate his humor.

Washington Irving was born on April 3, 1783, in New York City, then a town of about 25,000, part of whom were Dutch and part English. It was from this town that Irving drew much of the material for his stories and sketches. While a boy, he spent many hours with his dog and gun, rambling about the country regions that he later described in his stories. Sometimes he also wandered into the Dutch part of the city and listened to the quaint stories told by the Dutch descendants. At home he spent a great deal of time reading in his father's large library.

Irving was cheerful, kind, and sweet-natured, though a great part of his life was a struggle against ill health, grief, and work that he did not like. (The day had not yet come when an American author could hope to support himself by his writing alone, and there was no copyright law to protect his work.) He began the study of law, but his already delicate health was still further impaired by grief over the death of his fiancée. His family, therefore, sent him abroad, where he traveled throughout England, Holland, France, and Italy.

When he returned to America he wrote a humorous group of sketches titled *Salmagundi*. A little later his burlesque (a comedy filled with exaggeration meant to mock a person or idea) *History of New York from the Beginning of the World to the End of the Dutch Dynasty* appeared. Irving soon went abroad again on business for his brothers. This time he met many famous writers in England and gained new inspiration and encouragement.

Irving then set about writing in earnest. The first book he completed after his time in England was *The Sketch Book*. Sir Walter Scott helped him sell the book to an English publisher, and Irving received 2,000 dollars for it. *The Sketch Book* is the most widely known of Irving's works. It contains "Rip van Winkle"

A bust of novelist Washington Irving. The likeness once resided in New York City's Central and Prospect parks, but now stands in front of a high school named in Irving's honor. Latitudestock/Gallo Images/Getty Images

and "The Legend of Sleepy Hollow." In these he used the legends the descendants of the old Dutch settlers had told him—the mysterious tale of the return of Hendrick Hudson and his men and the ghost story of the headless horseman. Other charming sketches by Irving are the essays on Westminster Abbey and the Shakespeare country.

Irving remained abroad for many years, traveling, writing, and in the diplomatic service of his country. While minister to Spain in 1842 he became interested in Spanish history. His studies there furnished his lively imagination with plenty of material for *The Alhambra* and other works. The last 13 years of his life he spent at his home near Tarrytown on the Hudson, a region his pen made famous. He died on Nov. 28, 1859.

The first U.S. president elected after the Mexican-American War was a popular hero of that war, General Zachary Taylor. After more than 40 years in the army, Taylor became the first man to occupy the nation's highest office without previous political experience. The biggest problem he faced was how to organize the large Southwest Territory acquired from Mexico.

Taylor was born in Orange County, Va., on Nov. 24, 1784. A few months after his birth, his family moved across the Appalachian Mountains into what is now northern Kentucky. He grew up on his father's pioneer plantation in Jefferson County. There were no schools in the neighborhood, so Taylor received his only formal education from a private tutor.

Taylor enlisted in the army in 1806 and was commissioned first lieutenant in the infantry in 1808. During the next 40 years he served at several frontier posts and fought in the War of 1812, in Indian wars in the old Northwest Territory and Florida, and in the Mexican-American War. Among the men who served under him were Abraham Lincoln, in the Black

Hawk War, and Ulysses S. Grant and Jefferson Davis, in the Mexican-American War.

Taylor was an able and respected military commander. He wore a simple, informal uniform and in combat often exposed himself to enemy fire. His stocky build and stout endurance led his men to nickname him Old Rough and Ready.

In 1837 Taylor defeated the Seminole Indians in a bitter battle at Lake Okeechobee, Fla. He was then promoted to brigadier general. Three years later he became commander at Fort Smith, in Arkansas, and later Fort Jesup, in Louisiana. During this time he established a home in Baton Rouge, La.

Early in 1846, Taylor was ordered to occupy disputed territory between the Rio Grande and the Nueces River in what is now Texas. Both Mexico and the United States claimed this strip of land. The government of Mexico had previously been provoked by the annexation of Texas by the United States in 1845. On April 24, 1846, Taylor's troops clashed with Mexican soldiers. Old Rough and Ready immediately launched an attack that won the battles of Palo Alto and Resaca de la Palma. When Congress learned of the fighting it declared war on Mexico, on May 13, 1846.

In September 1846 Taylor defeated a large Mexican force at Monterrey, Mexico. Soon after, however, President James Polk sent General Winfield Scott to Mexico as chief American commander. Most of Taylor's troops were reassigned to Scott's command. Learning of Taylor's weakened position, Santa Anna, the Mexican commander, launched a powerful attack at Buena Vista. Despite a four-to-one superiority in numbers, the Mexicans were defeated on Feb. 23, 1847. This victory ended the war in northern Mexico and made Taylor a national hero.

In December 1847 Taylor returned to his Baton Rouge home to supervise his plantation. In 1848 the Whig Party nominated Taylor as its candidate for president. Taylor campaigned on his military record and his promise of a nonpolitical administration. Both the Whigs and the Democrats avoided the vital issue of the time—the expansion of slavery in the territories. As a result, most antislavery factions formed a Free Soil Party headed by former President Martin Van Buren.

Taylor defeated the Democratic candidate, Lewis Cass, in the general election, winning the electoral college vote 163–127. The Free Soilers failed to win an electoral vote, but the

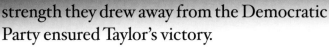

strength they drew away from the Democratic Party ensured Taylor's victory.

The greatest achievement of President Taylor's administration was in foreign affairs. In 1850 his secretary of state, John M. Clayton, arranged the Clayton-Bulwer Treaty with Great Britain. This agreement paved the way for the building of the Panama Canal half a century later.

At home the breach between the free and the slave states gradually widened. Although a slaveholder himself, Taylor opposed the unrestricted expansion of slavery. When California asked to be admitted as a free state, he recommended that Congress grant the request. Taylor also took a firm stand against Southern threats of secession from the Union.

In an effort to settle the sharp differences between the North and the South, Senator Henry Clay of Kentucky introduced eight compromise resolutions on Jan. 29, 1850. President Taylor favored changes in the original resolutions, but he died before such amendments could be made. On July 4, 1850, Taylor had laid a cornerstone for the Washington Monument. That night he became ill with cholera, and he died five days later, only 16 months after his inauguration.

The first American novelist to achieve worldwide fame was James Fenimore Cooper. His stories were translated into foreign languages as soon as they were published. Robert Louis Stevenson called him Cooper of the Wood and Wave because he wrote about American Indians and pioneers in the forest and sailors on the high seas.

James Fenimore Cooper was born in Burlington, N.J., on Sept. 15, 1789. When he was a year old the family moved to a large estate on Otsego Lake, N.Y. Here his father, William Cooper, laid out Cooperstown. The region was still a wilderness. Indians came to trade at the village.

In 1803 the younger Cooper went to Yale. He neglected his studies to spend most of his time outdoors and was expelled after three years. He went to sea for five years, first as a merchant sailor, then as a midshipman in the navy. In 1811 he married and went to live at his wife's home in Westchester County, N.Y.

Cooper's first novel, *Precaution*, was published in 1820. A story of English society life, it was a complete failure. The next year he turned to the American scene and won instant popularity with a Revolutionary War novel, *The Spy*. In 1823 Cooper wrote *The Pioneers*,

James Fenimore Cooper, author of the Leatherstocking Tales series of stories. **Hulton Archive/Getty Images**

the first of five Leatherstocking Tales. The intrepid scout Leatherstocking (sometimes called Natty Bumppo or Hawkeye) figures in all these stories. Cooper described him as "a philosopher of the wilderness, simple-minded, faithful, utterly without fear, and yet prudent." With the publication of *The Last of the Mohicans*, Cooper reached the height of his fame.

The novels in the Leatherstocking series are best read in the following order: *The Deerslayer* (1841), *The Pathfinder* (1840), *The Last of the Mohicans* (1826), *The Pioneers* (1823), and *The Prairie* (1827). The most popular of Cooper's sea stories are *The Pilot* (1823) and *The Red Rover* (1828).

In 1833, after spending years traveling abroad, Cooper settled on his estate in Cooperstown. He died there on Sept. 14, 1851.

CHAPTER 23

Often called the Father of Texas, Stephen F. Austin was responsible for settling thousands of American colonists in what was still part of Mexico. He also played a large role in the diplomatic activities that preceded Texan independence.

Stephen Fuller Austin was born on Nov. 3, 1793, in Austinville, Va. When he was 5 years old, the Austin family moved to Missouri. He later attended an academy in Connecticut and Transylvania University in Kentucky.

After losing his wealth in the Panic of 1819, Austin's father decided to reestablish himself by bringing American families into Texas. He died soon afterward, and his son took over the task. In 1821 Stephen Austin picked a site on the Brazos River for the first settlement. During the next 10 years he brought more than 5,000 settlers into Texas.

In 1833 Austin journeyed to Mexico City with the colonists' petition for a separate state government. Various difficulties led him to write a letter to the Texans urging them not to wait for approval but to go ahead

with their plans for a separate government. This letter was intercepted, and Austin was imprisoned until 1835.

Later that year, when Texas started to fight for independence, Austin was made the commander of the volunteer army. He left the army to win recruits and financial support in the United States. After independence had been won in 1836, he was defeated for the presidency of the new Republic of Texas by General Sam Houston, who appointed him secretary of state. Austin's health was broken, however, and he died on Dec. 27, 1836. The Texas republic's capital (now the state capital) was named in his honor.

The commander of the army that won the battle of San Jacinto—and Texas' independence—Sam Houston was twice elected president of the Republic of Texas. He also served Tennessee as a U.S. congressman and governor. When Texas became a state, Houston also served it as a U.S. senator and governor.

Samuel Houston was born in Rockbridge County, Va., on March 2, 1793. After his father died in 1807, his mother moved the family to a frontier farm in the Tennessee wilderness. Unwilling to work on the family farm or at the local store, Houston ran away in his mid-teens and lived with the neighboring Cherokee Indians for almost three years.

Houston volunteered for duty during the War of 1812, serving under Andrew Jackson against the Creek Indians. A good soldier, Houston was promoted to the rank of lieutenant. In 1814 he was wounded in battle at Horseshoe Bend, Ala.

In 1818 Houston returned to Tennessee and studied law. In his first year of practice

Army commander Sam Houston, who served as the first president of the Republic of Texas. **Stock Montage/Archive Photos/Getty Images**

he was elected district attorney. Aided by Jackson, he was appointed major general of the Tennessee militia in 1821. Two years later he was elected to Congress and served until 1827, upon which he became governor.

In 1829 Houston married, but the union soon ended in divorce, causing him to resign his office. He again sought refuge among the Cherokee and was formally adopted into the tribe. Several times he went to Washington, D.C., to fight for Native American rights. During this period Jackson sent him to Texas, then a Mexican province, to negotiate Indian treaties for the protection of U.S. border traders. There Houston became interested in the Texans' demand for separation from Mexico.

Houston established a home in Texas by 1833, and he quickly became one of the settlement's main leaders. When the settlers rose in rebellion against Mexico in November 1835, he was chosen commander-in-chief of their army. After a tough winter, on April 21, 1836, Houston and a force of roughly 800 Texans surprised and defeated 1,500 Mexicans under General Antonio López de Santa Anna at San Jacinto. This triumph secured Texan independence.

Houston was elected president of the new republic in 1836. After two years as president he served a term in the Texas congress, then, in 1841, became president again. He worked hard to have the United States annex Texas, a feat that was accomplished in 1845. In 1846 Houston was elected one of the new state's first two senators, serving until 1859, when he became governor. He fought unsuccessfully to prevent the secession of his state, and in March 1861 he was removed from office when he refused to swear allegiance to the Confederacy. He spent the next two years quietly at home in Texas with his second wife and mother of his eight children, whom he had married in 1840. Houston died on July 26, 1863, in Huntsville, Tex.

CHAPTER 25

The greatest American poet of the early 1800s was William Cullen Bryant. As a youth of 17 he wrote "Thanatopsis," a meditation on nature and death that remains his best-known poem. In the next 10 years he wrote "To a Waterfowl," "Green River," and "The Yellow Violet," nature lyrics that are well worth reading today. Bryant's busy life as a newspaper editor and publisher prevented him from further serious work as a poet, although he continued to publish occasional verse.

Bryant was born Nov. 3, 1794, in Cummington, Mass. His boyhood home in Cummington was surrounded by brooks, rivers, rocky hills, and woods. As a youth Bryant went fishing, gathered nuts and spearmint, and played in the fields. He attended the district schools until he was 12, then studied Latin and Greek. He spent a year in 1810-11 at Williams College.

In 1811 Bryant began to study law. He was admitted to the bar in 1815. Meantime he had already written "Thanatopsis" and "To a Waterfowl," and put them aside without

William Cullen Bryant. Encyclopædia Britannica, Inc.

thought of publication. A few years later Bryant's father found the poems and sent them to the *North American Review*, a popular monthly magazine. At once Bryant's genius was recognized. He was asked to contribute to magazines and invited to read the Phi Beta Kappa poem at the Harvard College commencement of 1821. That year he married Frances Fairchild.

In 1825 he moved to New York City to become editor of the *New York Review*. A year later he joined the *Evening Post*, a New York newspaper. From then on his time was taken up by editorial work. He gradually acquired a half interest in the paper. At first he stood with the Democrats on national affairs. Finally he broke with them on the slavery issue. When the Republican Party was formed in 1856 he rallied the paper to its cause. Bryant died in New York City on June 12, 1878.

The most effective slave revolt in U.S. history was led by a young black man, Nat Turner, who regarded himself as an agent of God to lead his people out of bondage. The revolt ended the false belief that slaves were either happy with their lives as they were or were too submissive to rebel.

Turner was born the property of a small plantation owner on Oct. 2, 1800, in Southampton County, Va. In the relatively easygoing atmosphere at this particular plantation, he was allowed to learn to read and write, and he hungrily absorbed much religious instruction as well. In the early 1820s he was sold to a nearby farmer, and again in 1831 to a craftsman named Joseph Travis.

By this time Turner's religion had become fanaticism. An eclipse of the sun in 1831 made him believe the time for insurrection had come. He planned to capture the armory at Jerusalem, the county seat. On August 21, with seven fellow slaves, he killed the Travis family. About 75 slaves rallied to his cause, and in the next two days 51 whites were murdered. The

An engraving showing 1830s slave-revolt leader Nat Turner confronting a white man with a rifle. Turner was eventually captured and executed for his role in the uprising. **Stock Montage/Archive Photos/ Getty Images**

revolt was handicapped, however, by a lack of discipline among Turner's followers and the fact that so few slaves turned out to help him. Armed resistance from whites, aided by

a 3,000-member force of state militia, ended the rebellion.

Most of the slaves were killed or captured. Turner escaped capture for six weeks but was finally caught, convicted, and hanged at Jerusalem on Nov. 11, 1831. His action subsequently set off a wave of legislation prohibiting the education, movement, and assembly of slaves. In 1832 *The Confessions of Nat Turner...as told to Thomas R. Grey* was published.

The leader of the Seminole Indians in their second war against the United States was Osceola. He was born about 1804 along the Tallapoosa River in Georgia. When he was 4 his family moved to Florida. As a boy he may have fought against Andrew Jackson in the First Seminole War.

In 1832 some Seminole chiefs signed a treaty that called for them to move to Indian Territory in present-day Oklahoma. Osceola and other young Seminoles opposed the move. In 1835 the Indian agent Wiley Thompson called a council at Fort Gibson. Some of the chiefs agreed to move. Osceola rose and plunged his dagger through the new treaty. He said, "This is the only treaty I will make with the whites!" He was then imprisoned. Later he pretended to favor the move and was released.

In December the conflict began. Osceola knew that the Indians were no match for the white soldiers in open battle, so he led the Seminoles deep into the Everglades. From there he led the Seminole braves in fierce raids on the white soldiers and settlers. The American public criticized the conduct of the war, and finally General T.S. Jesup was given 8,000 men to end it.

Some of the Seminole chiefs had given many braves as hostages for the move to Indian Territory. In June 1837 Osceola, with 200 warriors, liberated them and other Indians held by the army. In October, when Osceola came under a flag of truce to confer with one of Jesup's men, Jesup ordered him seized. Osceola was imprisoned first at St. Augustine, Fla. and later in Fort Moultrie in Charleston, S.C. He died on Jan. 20, 1838, and was buried with full military honors. The war dragged on until 1842, when most of the Seminole tribe surrendered and were moved to the West.

One of the earliest crusaders of the anti-slavery movement in the United States was William Lloyd Garrison. He helped found the Anti-Slavery Society and was its president for 23 years. For 35 years, until shortly after the Civil War, he published the violently antislavery weekly called the *Liberator*.

Garrison was born in Newburyport, Mass., on Dec. 10, 1805. When he was 13, he was apprenticed for seven years in the Newburyport *Herald* office. At 21 Garrison was editing the Newburyport *Free Press*. In it he published the earliest poems of John Greenleaf Whittier, who became his lifelong friend. After the paper failed, he went to Boston, where he helped edit the *National Philanthropist*, a paper devoted to moral reforms.

In 1829 Garrison gave his first address against slavery. That same year he went to Baltimore to help Benjamin Lundy edit an antislavery paper. One of his articles brought about his arrest for libel. Convicted, he served seven weeks of a jail term. On Jan. 1,

Abolitionist William Lloyd Garrison used the power of the press— his newspaper the Liberator—to voice his opinions on slavery. MPI/Archive Photos/Getty Images

1831, he began publishing the *Liberator*. In 1834 he married and lived in Roxbury, then a suburb of Boston. He had seven children, two of whom died in infancy.

Garrison traveled throughout the northern United States to make bitter attacks on slavery. He also went to England several times. The state of Georgia offered a reward for his arrest and conviction. In Boston a mob once placed a rope about his neck and forced him to parade down the street.

Garrison helped form antislavery societies, among them one in New England and the American Anti-Slavery Society. He preached that the North should secede from the South. In Boston in 1854 he publicly burned a copy of the U.S. Constitution, crying, "So perish all compromises with tyranny!"

After the Emancipation Proclamation of 1862, Garrison continued the *Liberator* for three more years until he could announce that "my vocation as an abolitionist is ended." In retirement he continued to champion the causes of temperance, women's rights, pacifism, and free trade. Weakened by ill health, Garrison died in New York City on May 24, 1879.

Two of the most vocal opponents of slavery and supporters of women's rights in the United States during the first half of the 19th century were sisters Sarah and Angelina Grimké. Although they came from the South, they took an early dislike to slavery. They eventually went North to become involved in the abolitionist movement, which aimed to end slavery.

Sarah Grimké was born on Nov. 26, 1792, and Angelina on Feb. 20, 1805, both in Charleston, S.C. Their father, a judge, had slaves. On visits to Philadelphia, Sarah became acquainted with the Society of Friends, or the Quakers, a religious group strongly opposed to slavery. In 1821 she left the South permanently and moved to Philadelphia to join the Quakers. Angelina followed in 1829.

In 1835 Angelina wrote a pro-abolitionist letter to William Lloyd Garrison, who published it in his newspaper, the *Liberator*. The next year she wrote a 36-page letter, "An Appeal to the Christian Women of the South," on the slavery issue. The same year

Sarah Grimké. **Fotosearch/Archive Photos/Getty Images**

Angelina Grimké. **Fotosearch/Archive Photos/Getty Images**

Sarah made a similar plea in "An Epistle to the Clergy of the Southern States." These and other appeals were warmly welcomed by the abolitionist crusaders in the North, but they brought forth a great deal of hostility in the South. In South Carolina officials burned copies of the letters and threatened the sisters with imprisonment if they ever returned to their native state.

The sisters' speaking career began when Angelina appeared before small groups of Philadelphia women in private homes. In 1836 the two moved to New York City and began addressing larger audiences in churches and public halls. These addresses aroused hostility among some men who believed that women had no right to preach. Thus, inadvertently,

Sarah and Angelina became pioneers in the early movement for women's rights in the United States.

In 1837 Angelina issued an "Appeal to the Women of the Nominally Free States." Sarah, in 1838, published "Letters on the Equality of the Sexes and the Condition of Woman."

In 1838 Angelina married the well-known abolitionist Theodore Dwight Weld. Ill health forced her to give up public speaking, and shortly afterward Sarah followed her into retirement. They settled in Hyde Park, now part of Boston, Mass. Sarah died there on Dec. 23, 1873, and Angelina on Oct. 26, 1879.

CHAPTER 30

An escaped slave, Frederick Douglass became one of the foremost black abolitionists and civil rights leaders in the United States. His powerful speeches, newspaper articles, and books awakened whites to the evils of slavery and inspired blacks in their struggle for freedom and equality.

Frederick Douglass was born Frederick Augustus Washington Bailey in Talbot County, Md., possibly in February 1818. His father was an unknown white man; his mother, Harriet Bailey, was a slave. He was separated from her and raised by her elderly parents.

When he was 7 years old Frederick was sent to his master, Captain Aaron Anthony, at a nearby plantation. There he first met a brother and two sisters. He later recalled sadly that "slavery had made us strangers."

The following year, Frederick became a servant to Hugh Auld, a relative of Captain Anthony who lived in Baltimore, Md. Frederick persuaded Auld's wife to teach him to read. But Auld believed slaves should not

Frederick Douglass went from being a slave to acting as an advisor to President Abraham Lincoln during the American Civil War. **Library of Congress Prints and Photographs Division**

be educated and stopped the lessons. White playmates helped Frederick, and he soon learned to read well. His reading of a book of speeches denouncing slavery and oppression deepened his hatred of slavery.

Upon Auld's death, Frederick was returned to the plantation as a field hand at 16. Later, he was hired out in Baltimore as a ship caulker. Frederick tried to escape with three others in 1833, but the plot was discovered before they could get away. Five years later, however, he fled to New York City and then to New Bedford, Mass., where he worked as a laborer for three years, eluding slave hunters by changing his surname to Douglass.

In 1841, at an antislavery convention, Douglass described his slave life in a moving speech that began his career as an abolitionist. From then on, despite heckling, mockery, insult, and violent personal attack, Douglass never flagged in his devotion to the abolitionist cause. Douglass became an agent of the Massachusetts Anti-Slavery Society, and in this capacity lectured to large assemblies. Many listeners were so impressed by Douglass' appearance and personality that they could not believe he had been a slave.

He had never revealed his former name or the name of his master.

To dispel doubts about his past, he published an autobiography in 1845, revised and completed in 1882 as *Life and Times of Frederick Douglass*. Fearful that it might lead to his reenslavement, Douglass fled to Great Britain, where he lectured to arouse support for the antislavery movement in the United States. English Quakers raised money to purchase his freedom, and in 1847 he returned home, now legally free.

That year, Douglass founded a new antislavery newspaper, the *North Star*—later renamed *Frederick Douglass's Paper*—in Rochester, N.Y. Unlike the abolition leader William Lloyd Garrison, Douglass had come to believe that political action, rather than moral persuasion, would bring about the abolition of slavery. Douglass also resented Garrison's view that blacks did not have the ability to lead the antislavery movement. By 1853, he had broken with Garrison and become a strong and independent abolitionist.

In 1859 Douglass refused to join the white abolitionist John Brown in his attempt to seize arms for a slave revolt from the federal arsenal at Harpers Ferry, W.Va. But Douglass did not reject violence as a weapon against slavery. He believed that "it can never be wrong for the imbruted and whip-scarred slaves, or their friends, to hunt, harass, and even strike down the traffickers in human flesh." Douglass was accused of helping Brown and was again forced to flee to England.

In the spring of 1860 he returned to the United States. During the Civil War, Douglass became a consultant to President Abraham Lincoln, advocating that former slaves be armed for the North and that the war be made a direct confrontation against slavery.

After the war, Douglass held several federal offices. In the District of Columbia he was appointed to the legislative council in 1871. He became a U.S. marshal there in 1877 and recorder of deeds in 1881. From 1889 to 1891 he served as minister to Haiti. Douglass fought for passage of the 15th Amendment to the Constitution—ratified in 1870—which gave blacks the right to vote. He died on Feb. 20, 1895, in Washington, D.C.

CONCLUSION

From the time George Washington took office as president in 1789 to the mid-point of the 19th century, the United States established itself as one of the great democracies of the world. The nation increased in population from less than 4 million to more than 23 million. At the same time it more than tripled its area to include almost 3 million square miles (7.8 million square kilometers). The growing strength of the nation was shown by the addition to the Union of 18 states. In 1789 there were 13 struggling states along the Atlantic seaboard. In 1850 the long expansion westward from the Atlantic coast to the Pacific coast was finally completed with the admission of California as the 31st state.

The continued growth of the nation, however, eventually led to sharp differences of opinion among the states on several issues, the most explosive of which was slavery. Although the founding fathers had succeeded in securing independence and bringing a dynamic new republic into existence, they left behind an ambiguous legacy with regard to slavery. Many of the founding fathers acknowledged that slavery violated the core American Revolutionary ideal of liberty. While gradually abolishing slavery in the North, however, they had permitted its rapid expansion in the South and Southwest.

The fears of many Southerners that Northern votes in Congress might exclude slavery in all the states were eased only temporarily by the Compromise of 1850. During the next 10 years, the issue of slavery and the related question of states' rights came to dominate the national debate, increasing the tension between the North and the South and leading ultimately to the outbreak of the nation's deadliest conflict, the American Civil War.

annexation The act of officially making a territory part of an existing state or nation.

audacity Bold disregard of normal restraints.

charter A grant or guarantee of rights, franchises, or privileges from the sovereign power of a state or country.

commission The assigning of a special task, or being given official powers to perform a task.

Federalist A member of a major political party in the early years of the United States favoring a strong centralized national government.

insurrection Rising up against authority, particularly an established government.

malevolent Having, showing, or arising from intense often vicious ill will, spite, or hatred.

militia A part of the organized armed forces of a country liable to call only in emergency.

munitions Fortification built and ammunition gathered for defense against an enemy.

nullification The action of a state impeding or attempting to prevent the operation and enforcement within its territory of a law of the United States.

privateer An armed private ship licensed to attack enemy shipping.

quell To calm or make quiet.

ratification The act of approving and sanctioning formally.

repeal To make a law or ruling obsolete by legislative action.

secession Formal withdrawal from an organization or country.

sedition Speaking or acting out against a country's government to the point of starting a rebellion or riot.

shrewd Being very aware of a situation and capable of sharp thinking.

stalwart Marked by outstanding strength and vigor of body, mind, or spirit.

surveyor One who studies Earth's surface and measures positions, points, and lines, usually in order to help establish boundaries or make maps.

American Historical Association (AHA)
400 A Street, SE
Washington, DC 20003
(202) 544-2422
Web site: http://www.historians.org
The AHA serves as a leader and advocate for
    professionals, researchers, and students in
    the field of history and upholds academic
    and professional standards. The AHA also
    awards a number of fellowships and prizes
    and offers important resources and publi-
    cations for anyone interested in the field.

The Gilder Lehrman Institute of American
    History
19 West 44th Street, Suite 500
New York, NY 10036
(646) 366-9666
Web site: http://www.gilderlehrman.org
The Gilder Lehrman Institute of American
    History is a nonprofit organization that
    offers a wide range of programs and
    resources for students and history enthu-
    siasts throughout the nation. Among their
    programs are print and digital publications,
    essay contests, traveling exhibitions, and a
    lecture series featuring eminent historians.

Miller Center
2201 Old Ivy Road
Charlottesville, VA 22904
(434) 924-7236
Web site: http://millercenter.org
The Miller Center at the University of
Virginia furthers understanding of all
aspects of the presidency, political history,
and policy through various research ini-
tiatives, programs, events, and fellowship
opportunities.

National Museum of American History
(NMAH)
14th Street and Constitution Avenue, NW
Washington, DC 20002
(202) 633-1000
Web site: http://americanhistory.si.edu
With over three million artifacts of American
history in its collection, many of which
are on display, the NMAH is a dedicated
to promoting public interest in the events
that shaped the American nation.

Organization of American Historians (OAH)
112 North Bryan Avenue
Bloomington, Indiana 47408

(812) 855-7311

Web site: http://www.oah.org

Committed to advancing scholarship in the field of American history, the OAH supports a number of programs, publications, and resources for students, teachers, researchers, and professionals in the field.

WEB SITES

Due to the changing nature of Internet links, Rosen Educational Services has developed an online list of Web sites related to the subject of this book. This site is updated regularly. Please use this link to access the list:

http://www.rosenlinks.com/ioacb/newambio

BIBLIOGRAPHY

Adler, David A. *Frederick Douglass: A Noble Life* (Holiday House, 2010).

Ambrose, Stephen E. *Undaunted Courage: Meriwether Lewis, Thomas Jefferson, and the Opening of the American West* (Simon & Schuster, 1996).

Beyer, Mark. *The War of 1812: The New American Nation Goes to War with England* (Rosen Publishing, 2004).

Burns, James MacGregor, and Dunn, Susan. *George Washington* (Times Books, 2004).

Corps, Terry. *Historical Dictionary of the Jacksonian Era and Manifest Destiny* (Scarecrow Press, 2006).

DeKeyser, Stacy. *Sacagawea* (Franklin Watts, 2004).

Fradin, Dennis B. *The Trail of Tears* (Marshall Cavendish Benchmark, 2008).

Hammond, John Craig, and Mason, Matthew. *Contesting Slavery: The Politics of Bondage and Freedom in the New American Nation* (University of Virginia Press, 2011).

Meacham, Jon. *American Lion: Andrew Jackson in the White House* (Random House, 2008).

Morgan, Edmund S. *American Heroes: Profiles of Men and Women Who Shaped Early America* (W.W. Norton & Co., 2009).

INDEX